ПРИКАЗНАТА ЗА БРОЕВИ

THE NUMBER STORY

SMALL BOOK ONE

ENGLISH – MACEDONIAN

Numbers Teach Children
Their Number Names

written and illustrated by

MISS ANNA

Early Reader Edition of *The Number Story 1*
Bronze Medal Winner, 2016 Wishing Shelf Book Award

Library of Congress Control Number: 2018902040

Names: Miss Anna, author.
Title: Number story : numbers teach children their number names / Miss Anna.
Description: Portland, OR: Lumpy Publishing, 2018.
Identifiers: ISBN 978-1-945977-45-9 | LCCN 2018902040
Summary: The pictures and rhymes present stories which introduce numbers 0-10.
Subjects: LCSH Numeration—English--Macedonian--Pictorial works--Juvenile literature. | BISAC JUVENILE NONFICTION /
Languages: English--Macedonian
Classification: LCC QA141.3 .M57 2018 | DDC 513—dc23

Publisher: Lumpy Publishing
Website: www.missannabooks.com
Email: missanna@missannabooks.com

Paperback: ISBN 978-1-945977-45-9
Printed in the U.S.A.   1 3 5 7 9 10 8 6 4 2

Сакате ли да учиме
имиња на бројки?

It is very easy and a lot of fun!

Многу е лесно, и забавно многу!

Say-along our little jingle

Запејте мала приказна со нас!

starting from Number One!

Ќе почнеме со бројката еден!

ONE looks like my one finger.

ЕДЕН

Личи на мојот прст еден.

ONE!
ЕДЕН!

2

TWO trails a tail.

ДВА

следи опашка.

A TAIL! ОПАШКА!

3

THREE has bumps.

ТРИ

има цумки.

BUMPY!   ЦУМКИ!

4

A SAIL!
ЕДРО!

5

FIVE is a racing track.

ПЕТ

е тркачка патека.

VROOM
БРРРРМ!
1

SIX   curves like a snail.

ШЕСТ

Се врти ко полжав.

A SNAIL! ПОЛЖАВ!

7

SEVEN has a sharp angle.

СЕДУМ

со остра ивица.

OUCH!
АУЧ!

8

EIGHT is rollercoaster rails.

ОСУМ

Се шини за ролеркостер.

JEJ!
YIPPEE!

9

NINE   is a bubble on a stick.

ДЕВЕТ

е меурче на стапче.

A BUBBLE! МЕУРЧЕ!

TEN   is an eye of a whale.

ДЕСЕТ

Е едно око на кит.

WINK!

Ви намигна!

And
И

0

ZERO   is an empty pail.

НУЛА

е празна шина.

IT'S EMPTY!
Празна е!

Thank you for playing with us today.

We had a lot of fun too!

Благодариме што поигравте со нас.

И нам ни беше забавно!

We are your Number friends,
Zero to Ten,
Who will be here for you~

Ние сме вашите Бројки пријатели
Нула до Десет.
Ќе бидеме секогаш тука за вас!

Bye-bye now!
See you again soon!

Чао-чао сега!

Се гледаме наскоро пак!

The Numbers are *SINGING* too!

To sing-a-long, look for Miss Anna Number Story
at your favorite music store like iTUNES.

MP3

Numbers 0-10
IDENTIFYING & COUNTING

Numbers 11-20
& Ordinals
first, second, third...

Numbers 0-100
& Place Values
ones, tens, hundreds...

About Clocks
& Telling Time
hours, minutes, seconds

Number Story 1 & 2
isbn: 978-0-996216-48-7

Number Story 3 & 4
isbn: 978-1-945977-01-5

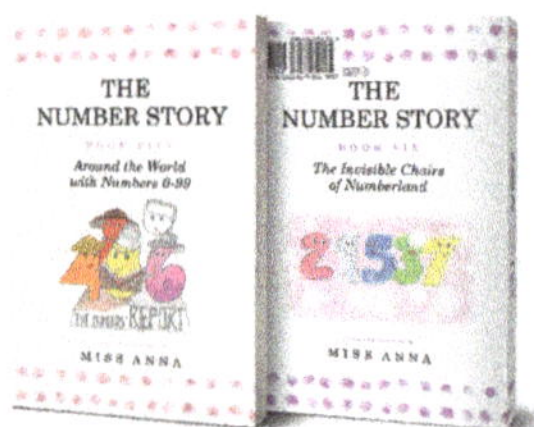

Number Story 5 & 6
isbn: 978-1-945977-06-0

Number Story 7 & 8
isbn: 978-1-949320-40-4

For more Miss Anna books to love,
visit us at

www.missannabooks.com

Numbers are working hard all over the world!
Come Travel the World with Us!